aquarius

january 21 ◆ february 19

WHITE STAR PUBLISHERS

contents

Text by
Patrizia Troni

Graphic Design
Maria Cucchi

Character and Temperament

The Aquarius character can be summed up in the following concept: absolute need for space and freedom. Freedom of movement and ideas. Freedom of initiative and freedom to express their viewpoint no matter what, without having to be subjected to another's opinion. They are the sign with the most need for self-reliance and independence. And although they respect the rules of the civilized world, those rules must never become a restriction, a cage, torture.

There are two clear-cut aspects of the Aquarius lifestyle. On the one hand, the necessity of constructing a stable, solid role in the world, not so much due to excessive ambition or vanity, but because such a role protects them from the risk of having to be under someone else's control. While practical, everyday life is fine and is no problem for them, one could be even freer. On the other hand, this respect for roles must never go so far as to trap them in a corner, be an obligation, to suffocate them.

Side by side with the concept of freedom and the absolute need for independence are two other factors that are indispensable for their happiness: movement and transformation. They must be as far away as possible from boring habits and repetitive acts and must live in the midst of vivacious company.

Aquarius is one of the most sociable signs in the Zodiac. They like to float from one situation to the next, always keeping the entrance and exit doors open. Because their open-mindedness is also mental and ideological, it cannot be enclosed in a circle that blocks movement in all directions. And, just as they demand freedom for themselves, equally they respect the freedom of others. They leave their house door open because they want the world to enter and exit freely, like the wind, enjoying open space to the utmost.

Aquarius is the wind that moves lightly and ethereally, sometimes almost without even leaving a trace behind them. They are not conceited or conditioned by an ego that continuously needs to be acknowledged. They prefer a collective vision in which individualism is not tantamount to domination and arrogance but is, rather, the possibility for all to realize themselves – free and liberal, emancipated, without any fixed priority impediments. With Aquarius, all things are possible. They do not like insistent, tenacious bonds, intrusiveness, being conditioned and having to tolerate platitudes. They are original and non-conformist. They adore surprises and amazement, and detest foregone conclusions and predictability, everything always remaining the same. They pursue change and evolution, because for them life is in motion. Aquarius does not like opinions carved in stone, the stubbornness of those who are convinced they are always right. For Aquarius, existence is an uninterrupted flow, an adventure to be enjoyed in a detached, light-hearted way.

Routine is their worst enemy, and they do not dwell in the past. Aquarius lives in the present.

For Aquarius, life must be a constant path of new experiences. Novelty excites them, while they are depressed by sameness and monotony. They were not made for clear and definite forms, because being open-minded and receptive also means loving diversity and variety.

Their motto is "down with boredom". Aquarius loves to surprise and be surprised, and, especially, enjoy invisibility, sudden disappearance that is nothing more or less than a clear message for the whole world: don't make me always be the same and live the same way.

Love and Passion

8 Aquarius

Aquarius wants to be free even where love is concerned. Reassuring, ingrained, routine, boring, suffocating and possessive love that conditions and smothers, that ends up becoming mere habit without that exciting stimulus that catches one off guard, is definitely not for them. No, they prefer an open relationship based on understanding, sincere dialogue and the possibility of both partners to feel free and to move in whatever direction they want without being hampered by a sense of obligation. Thus, love becomes almost a friendship, in which the partners understand one another and respect one another's personality without either wanting to impose their will or lord it over the other.

If life is something that flows in splendid ease, then it follows that love must also be a captivating, exciting adventure that stirs the mind instead of dampening it; it must enhance the taste for exploration and adventure that often triggers strong imagination, and encompass the pleasure of transgression, and the bizarre, that become the basis of an even more profound accord.

This rejection of the over-traditional couple, and this need for freedom and independence, even on the part of the female Aquarius (it must be said that women born under this sign are the prototype of progres-

siveness and emancipation), could lead to romantic feeling becoming idealized or even to an impossible love.

Aquarius is often found in situations that are somewhat strange, that deviate from the rigorous lines of the norm. On the one hand, while idealization, and impossible or irregular love have their limits - because in order for the idea and dream to remain such, they must never be fully realized - on the other hand they allow the couple to maintain that spirit of independence and personal freedom of action and movement that they simply cannot do without.

For Aquarius, love and passion must stir the imagination that takes them to other worlds, that frees them from identities that are too anchored, in a context of magic and surprise, which it will be wonderful to break loose from. Therefore, passion is something that may suddenly burst into flame, that nourishes itself on flashes of lightning, circumstances that may be somewhat sophisticated, with exquisite taste for forms and beauty that is married to the pleasure of intelligent repartee, rapid and passionate verbal fencing. This includes erotic departures that can be shared, most pleasurably, with a partner, in whom one has absolute trust and from whom one expects absolute trust.

Love consists of a thousand levels and a thousand worlds, and is not a maelstrom that first attracts Aquarius and then entangles them for eternity. This is not to say that there can be no projects or plans in matters of love, quite the contrary. But, they pop up in a flash and Aquarius wants to carry them out immediately. It is also true that life for Aquarius is made up of a great many projects, and when their partner is not as adaptable as they are, a new objective may replace the former one, which is no longer interesting. Their partner must be as flexible as they are, and receptive to the idea of passing through scores of universes together. However, should this accord become too much of a habit, or should a partner suffocate them, then Aquarius will you soon fly the coop.

For Aquarius, love, like life itself, is perennial experimentation, without exaggerated manifestations of tenderness, without too much jealousy, which they simply cannot bear. Love means dialogue, sharing and accord, with light-hearted and very vivacious communication with one's partner, and always with that touch of eccentricity and creativity that guarantees that true love will not become either an obsession or drab banality made up of rites that are always humdrum, always identical.

How to Hook an Aquarius and How to Let Them Go

Whoever wants to hook an Aquarius must bear in mind that they cannot tolerate having someone always underfoot, suffocating them and embroiling them in obligations and duties. Love for Aquarius means freedom, variety, and transformation. Habit is tantamount to horror. As we know, Aquarius loves to surprise and be surprised. With this sign, one must be prepared for intense passion garnished with small doses of madness, eccentricity and bizarre variations, sudden changes and novelties. The Aquarius male is restless and unpredictable, and in order to seduce him one must play with him as a cat plays with a mouse – appear and disappear, take him and leave him. To win his heart, one must avoid making him feel secure and, above all, absolutely avoid running after him. He wants a woman who is witty, and independent, not possessive, a woman who is in harmony with him, intellectually. For Aquarius, dialogue is indispensable, just as it is important to share fantasies, even non-conformist ones, and a host of emotions.

Playing hard to get is a useful way of winning the heart of the Aquarius female, who prefers to pursue rather than to be pursued. You must not give her the impression of your having been captivated by her fascination, because if a man runs after her she will surely drive him crazy. If, on the other hand, he seems to be eluding her she will be the one to go crazy. The Aquarius female loves a difficult conquest, the uncatchable man, the prey who slips out of her clutches. For her, love is freedom. She is emancipated, self-reliant, and wants a man who is flexible, intelligent, and tender but, above all, a friend. Aquarius is the master of the disappearing act, but it is not advisable for you to do the same. If you must leave them, suddenly disappearing would only make them even more attached to you. It would be best to talk to them calmly, explaining that you want to break off the relationship because love has become mere friendship.

Compatibility with Other Signs

The best and liveliest relationships for Aquarius bloom with two Air signs, Gemini and Libra. With those born under these signs, the accord is spontaneous, natural and immediate, often giving rise to a deep common affection that eliminates the confines between love and friendship. With a Libra or Gemini partner, Aquarius makes a sophisticated, handsome, and dazzling couple that knows the ways of the world and is, in turn, admired and envied by the world. Felicitous professional and business agreements and alliances can occur between Aquarius and Aries and Sagittarius. The Aquarius astuteness does a lot of good to, and goes well with, these two Fire signs, which are at times too impulsive and not opportunistic enough. And, romantic relationships with them prove to be quite good. The sunny, open, vital character of these signs blends well with the expansive Aquarius nature.

A partnership where both are Aquarius makes for an idealistic, altruistic couple. Common interests, shared trips, sensations and ideals cement their romance. However, perfect harmony is achieved only when they have similar wavelengths. Saturn and Uranus rule Aquarius: one of couple might, therefore, be ruled by Saturn (serious and rational) and the other by Uranus (inventive and transgressive). When both are ruled by Uranus then the result is folly and open sociability, while if both are ruled by Saturn it makes for an exemplary couple with great intellectual harmony. But, this harmony falters if one is ruled by Saturn and the other by Uranus. Theoretically, with Taurus and Leo there is no exceptional meeting ground, since the former is too fascinating and the latter too static. There is a strong, palpable and powerful attraction with Scorpio, Pisces and Cancer. Relationships with these signs produce games of seduction made up of long anxious waits, provocations, quick departures and lies that drive Aquarius crazy.

Fundamentally, Virgo and Capricorn do not understand Aquarius and are not always able to bear their sparkling spirit. Their secure, calm and judicious character is good for Aquarius, but the relationship risks sinking into sheer boredom.

Aquarius Profession and Career

In the sphere of work, eventually there emerges the Aquarius need for freedom and independence, for transformation and change. Because if, as they claim, life is a state of becoming and development and has always been part of a process of endless change, in their workplace they also want variety, or at least the possibility to have a job that does not oblige them to stay in an office from morning to evening, surrounded by the usual faces and duties.

The Aquarius need for new experiences is linked to the great sociability of their character. Therefore, an ideal job for Aquarius would entail either something to do with traveling or something with continuous contact with different people.

Certainly, the field of communication is very suitable. Aquarius has a gift for making contact with different people and establishing ongoing relationships, and making others feel at ease, as well as understanding what can be useful and advantageous. Aquarius is a great diplomat and knows how to maintain relationships, even with a good dose of healthy opportunism that is combined with their excellent capacity to understand another's soul and to act with perfect timing.

When it comes to teamwork, Aquarius can be exceptional, cooperative and constructive. They feel comfortable working with and in a group and are skilled at creating the ideal working conditions for others. Often, Aquarius is comfortable in the midst of frenetic social activity; consequently, they would be suitable for organizing public events.

Although Aquarius is able to maintain the appearance of bourgeois decorum necessary in an important professional role, their inventive and creative nature loves novelty and discovery. They are not only eminently suited as first-rate organizers of events, etc., salesmen and masters of public relations, but could also be inventors, discoverers – in other words, geniuses capable of realizing an unexpected breakthrough that can greatly improve work procedures and conditions.

Aquarius includes fine experts in the fields of technology and electronics, but their skill in establishing immediate contact with others, and their sensitivity, makes them excellent physicians who introduce the quality of a new perspective, often different from prevailing cultural models and presenting alternative cures.

Aquarius is also a master at creating a host of projects and continuously proposing new business ideas that, at that moment, enthuse and excite them but then may be suddenly abandoned. What they like

about dreaming up projects is the flash of creation, the idea itself. When it comes to putting the idea into practice, they are less enthusiastic and committed. They like to experiment and their natural technical and mathematical skill has produced many experts in engineering, mathematics, physics and finance. In the workplace, Aquarius wants a co-operative atmosphere. They are not the type who forges ahead alone or who isolates themselves from the context. They make others feel at ease, putting themselves on the others' level, thus revealing great flexibility and adaptability, virtues that make it possible for Aquarius to smooth out moments of tension that might arise.

Although Aquarius certainly does not disdain the role of the entre-preneur - which they are quite capable of carrying out with fresh ideas and surprising flashes of ingenuity - they do not like to be burdened with responsibility and expectation, because they prefer to be their own boss, as it were, without having to answer to others for their decisions.

What freethinking and slightly rebellious people, like Aquarius, cannot bear is authoritarianism as an end in itself. An office manager or supervisor who treats Aquarius arrogantly and condescendingly will soon have to deal with their spirit, which cannot stand being dominated or humiliated.

How an Aquarius Thinks and Reasons

No one should underestimate the extremely brilliant Aquarius intelligence, because it has a two-fold quality that is very rarely seen in other signs. Aquarius is capable of both lightning intuition and cold strategic vision. They grasp the invisible, profound meaning between the lines and even between one word and the next, that indefinable something that may be revealed by a tiny detail. They are blessed with uncommon discernment and sensitivity in grasping what is subtle, but unlike others who lack comprehension – in other words, who are only emotional and intuitive, only ingenious and hence, basically, irrational – they are able to combine their subtle, rapid vision with reasoning that can evaluate dispassionately by detaching itself from things, a kind of cool objectivity that allows them to avoid being influenced by what they are viewing and trying to grasp.

This logic is coupled with the capacity to penetrate another's subconscious. This is possible, partly, because they are subtle observers who appreciate forms, especially those with something that deviates from the norm, so much so that they can understand people by studying the way they talk, how they express themselves, move about, dress and behave.

In short, Aquarius goes straight to the heart of the matter right away, being deep thinkers as well as excellent observers. This is the reason why their diagnoses and conclusions are so often correct. It is as if they had a tiny, invisible laser that they use to grasp the souls of other people.

But, there is another aspect to be added to these qualities, in the way they use their intellect: the gift of extraordinary imagination that makes them among the most brilliant and surprising of people. They are ingenious, inventive; they do not limit themselves to mere facts, nor do they limit reality to what it is. Indeed, after viewing reality they want to transform it, renew it, offer an interpretation, add a new connotation and an original perspective.

If their intelligence must have a defect, it is sometimes that of not having the patience to delve, study in depth, or dissect, because they become easily bored and attracted by something else, by a new world they have entered and with which they must become thoroughly acquainted.

Aquarius is somewhat inconsistent and erratic, partly because the same fine insight that helps them to grasp the essence, the basic truth, of the minutest detail, also leads them to lose interest.

The same holds true as regards their intellectual passions or their other interests and hobbies. They often start off with great enthusiasm, almost as if they were prey to a form of rapturous excitement; then, suddenly, there is a total lack of interest and they drop everything on the spot, going on to be captivated by a new, and overwhelming passion.

The idealistic undercurrent in the Aquarius character is also one of the causes of their frequent, likeable bouts of utopian fervor, which aims to chang the world radically, supported by many good intentions, but is not always followed by consistent and firm action. At times, this aspect of the Aquarius nature bewilders others, who are amazed at the fact that Aquarius has suddenly had a change of mind and is immediately ready to revolutionize something else.

Aquarius is curious, intelligent and brilliant, with an open-minded and truly libertarian mentality. Even in their mode of reasoning, thinking and understanding there emerges that anarchical and rebellious streak, manifested from one moment to the next, which makes Aquarius truly unique.

Sociability, Communicatior

and Friendship

For Aquarius, sociability and communication are the basic conditions for them to be in harmony with their spirit and character. For them, being sociable means the pleasure of mingling with people, becoming acquainted with more and more people, making friends and seeing old friends with whom they can share ideas, feelings and experiences. They are so sociable partly because they are able to deal with matters by themselves and can count on their own eminently independent spirit, because others must never condition, lead or dominate them.

Being in company excites Aquarius because one aspect of their curious and extrovert character is that they are aware that the world is full of acquaintances and knowledge. Their scintillating and extrovert nature overcomes boredom, drabness, and the always-identical routine of life. They are social creatures because they think it is something worthwhile, not so much for motives of base opportunism, but because mankind's social dimension is a bulwark against dangerous individualist excesses. In fact, for Aquarius, the expression "in unity lies strength" is extremely pertinent. But, being with others in the fiery whirlwind of events, some of which are surprising, is also enjoyable for Aquarius, it makes them merry and lends a touch of unpredictability to everyday life, which would be empty and sad were they all alone. This does not mean that they do not enjoy moments of solitude, but they are at their ease in company and are in agreeable high spirits both in familiar company, in which there is a certain playful atmosphere, and with new acquaintances.

In this sense, since ancient times astrological tradition has considered Aquarius the sign of friendship. Being a friend to Aquarius does not mean having passed a rigorous selection test that the mistrustful might prepare themselves for before opening the doors to their hearts. It is the very becoming of life that continuously gives rise to accord and harmony, which is almost immediate but, at the same time, profound and which, in turn, soon triggers some kind of useful and profitable cooperation (Aquarius has a practical sense here even where friendship is concerned).

Those who interact with Aquarius, share time, projects and a certain daily routine with them, are already friends, without having to demonstrate any strong feelings.

Aquarius is accused of being an opportunistic sign, but for them, someone is a friend not just because they are useful or helpful. No, a friend is a friend because of shared emotions and experiences, and Aquarius always has the utmost respect for another's personality.

Favorite friends are those who share a delight in play, confidence, with a light and easy touch. In other words, those with whom Aquarius can have a relationship that is not heavy-handed and does not take on dramatic tones, but flows effortlessly, leaving a sensation of extraordinary reciprocal freedom that allows both parties to express themselves openly, without too many inhibitions, secrets or complications. Aquarius does not choose friends who condition or stifle them, nor to use as confidants or for a shoulder to cry on. In fact, Aquarius rarely uses friends as confessors or psychiatrists. For Aquarius, with their true friends there is almost no need for words; one simply takes off on a trip, shares an adventure or even a transgressive act, and that's that.

Aquarius is a sign of friendship, and, traditionally, Aquarius often has influential friends, so that it is not difficult for them to find support and establish alliances and sincere, disinterested relationships.

When Aquarius Gets Angry

All astrology manuals point out that Aquarius is a sign of friendship. Friendship is fundamental for Aquarius, but it must be based upon the greatest freedom and open-mindedness. For Aquarius, the rule of friendship is that there must no rules. If a friend creates difficulties for Aquarius, tries to control them, or becomes inflexible or irritating, then Aquarius will cut them off without delay. Because Aquarius is diplomatic, they do not like to raise their voice, preferring to moderate, tone down, or even slip away rather than become temperamental. In fact, they are adept at disappearing when the atmosphere becomes heavy or the situation tight, and they are masters at not tackling things head on, letting tension fade away gradually.

Aquarius has a deep-seated open-mindedness. Prejudices, the status quo, biases, clichés and hackneyed phrases all make Aquarius angry. For Aquarius, life is an exchange of ideas, opinions, and knowledge that are transformed without settling stubbornly on one point. Aquarius cannot contemplate just a single idea, a single perspective. They do not accept dogma and they question everything, which is the reason why they are annoyed by people who cling stubbornly to a single idea, by those who view life from just one point of view and believe in things that they have never experienced. Aquarius cannot accept static ideologies, fanaticism, those who want to impose their viewpoint. Equally irritating for Aquarius are those who are too sure of themselves, presumptuous, braggarts and egocentric. But, what angers Aquarius the most are arrogant, overbearing people who are convinced that they have a monopoly on the truth and who want to impose it on others.

Aquarius is a sign of anarchy; they find it hard to bear those who abuse their power, dominate everything and, instead of asking, take command and exert control.

Aquarius
Children

It is easy to adore the Aquarius child. They are sociable, vivacious, interested in the world about them, and full of curiosity. They have a vivid imagination and a capacity for abstraction, which leads them to experience life and existence as a continuous adventure, full of surprises. The fact that they are never still, either physically or mentally, might make one think that they are always getting into mischief, but we must bear in mind their superior intellect, sense of opportunism and special intuition, all of which keeps them away from people or things that might be harmful.

They know how to avoid complications and trouble and they have an innate talent for slipping out of uncomfortable situations. They are also very clever at eluding questions that they don't want to answer, but not because they are evasive or liars. While one must admit that Aquarius has a certain tendency to bend the truth to suit their desires, it is also true that a white lie or an omission often occurs due to their innate diplomatic nature, which compels them to respect others' sensitivities. Their parents must realize that they do not always say what they think and do not always think what they say.

Aquarius is ruled by Saturn and Uranus, which can create a character that is more ruled by either Saturn (in which case we have a child who wants to make a good impression, has a sense of duty and rarely goes to extremes) or by Uranus (in which case we have a child who is a non-conformist, imaginative and very idealistic).

Whether Saturn or Uranus prevails, the Aquarius child is like a little bird that becomes sad if put in a cage. They want to be free from commitments and constriction, and be able to move about freely. It is up to their parents to embrace them with intelligence and love, educate them and give them solid rules without ever making them feel forced to do anything or to act in a particular way.

Music Associated

Many great musicians, composers and singers were born under Aquarius. For Aquarius, music is a fundamental art form. Not only do they like to listen to it, but also to play and produce it themselves. Aquarius is known for rare musical ability and virtuosity and for explosive and overwhelming spirit, which never stops once it begins to create, and is always searching for techniques and solutions that will surprise and amaze. It is no accident that Aquarius can boast such eternal classical music figures as Mozart and Schubert, eclectic and highly sensitive, master composers, geniuses with the talent and propensity for exploring and attempting ever-new compositional procedures. Virtuosity, however, is not the primary characteristic of Aquarius musicians and composers; it is creating music with a new atmosphere that captures the listener, creating a totally new musical perspective. As for the 20th century, mention must be made of the great Spanish tenor Plácido Domingo and the violinist Uto Ughi. In the world of

with Aquarius

rock music, there are many interpreters in the limelight thanks to their transgressive spirit, their assault on rules and on preceding styles. The great reggae star, Bob Marley, is flanked by such luminaries as Alice Cooper, Justin Timberlake and two of the English musicians who founded Genesis, Peter Gabriel and Phil Collins. Genesis exemplifies the magical and psychedelic spirit typical of Aquarius, which in literature brought fame to the author of *Alice in Wonderland*, Lewis Carroll. The American singers Amii Stewart and Axl Rose, and the British singer Mark Owen, also belong to Aquarius, as do Robbie Williams, Alicia Keys, Shakira, Natalie Imbruglia, and Vasco Rossi. One instrument that is in harmony with Aquarius is the electric guitar.

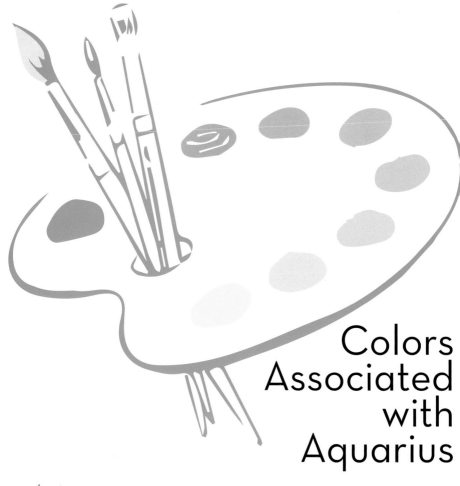

Colors
Associated
with
Aquarius

The vivacity of yellow and the passion of red are combined to create the Aquarius color, orange. This bright, sparkling, flamboyant color expresses the spontaneous Aquarius nature, the lightness of spirit that makes Aquarius soar and the total open-minded approach it has with respect to the world.

Orange is a warm, fascinating color that stimulates spirituality, as well as sexual desire. It symbolizes the quest for equilibrium between spirit and libido, represents passion, the vital drive that rouses and stirs Aquarius, its courageous, totally engrossing faith in life. This is the color of Aquarius because Aquarius plunges, body and soul, into things, in the universes of sociability and life without prejudices or silly preclusions.

Orange is the color of the tunic of the Muses and of Buddhist monks. In the Hindu religion, it stands for asceticism, abstention from indulgence in material things, while for the early Christians it symbolized the sin of gluttony. In ancient Rome, on the other hand, it was the color of love, because women's bridal veil, the *flammeum*, was orange. Therefore, this color expresses both pure, divine, idealized love, and lust, excess and debauchery (Dionysus, the god of winemaking and ecstasy, wore orange garments).

For Aquarius, choose a hue of bright orange to feel the need for emotion, if in need of something new and to meet a challenge, to risk, take a gamble. It is a tone that helps one to emerge from shadow and imparts well-balanced energy and playful sensuality. Cadmium orange is a warm hue that helps to finish projects and to choose the right approach or vision, or to make the right decision, because it imparts more lucidity to one's mind. Choose a pleasant carrot orange, if there is no desire whatsoever to be suffocated by duties and no need to abstain from pleasure. This tone transmits enthusiasm, which in turn makes Aquarius vital and communicative.

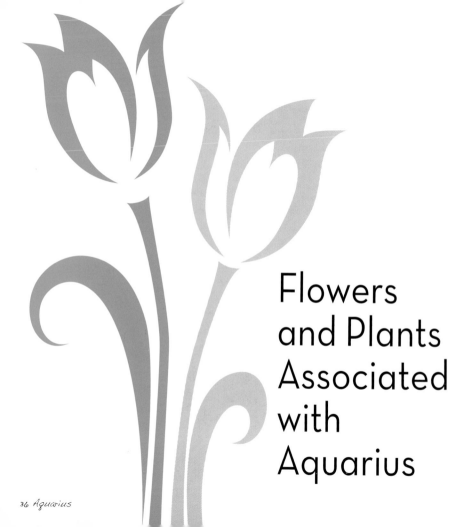

Flowers
and Plants
Associated
with
Aquarius

When the Sun enters Aquarius, spring is in the air. It is still cold at night, but the days begin to become longer and the light more intense. The snowdrop is the flower of Aquarius because it is the first to bloom, much like a portent of the coming spring. Traditionally, it is believed that gathering a snowdrop at night with a full moon will make one happy all year long. This flower is connected to Icarus (the mythological figure associated with Aquarius): according to an ancient Greek legend, when spring arrives the wind mourns for the death of the young Icarus and its tears, penetrating the earth, are transformed into the white snowdrop shoots. Other flowers associated with Aquarius are the geranium, the sumptuous bougainvillea, the amaryllis and the dahlia.

The following flowers and plants are associated with each ten-day period.

First period (January 21-30): fern. For those who belong to this period, walking every so often in ferny undergrowth will fill them with energy. But, fern also thrives in an apartment. Having this plant nearby helps an idealistic and imaginative sign like Aquarius to detach itself just enough from things in order to evaluate them with the right amount of objectivity.

Second period (January 31–February 9): lily of the valley. This flower favors change and rouses those who have been inactive for too long. It is beneficial for those born in this ten-day period, as well as for those who live with them: the flowers, and the essence, of lily of the valley should be placed under a partner's pillow to shake them out of becoming too boring and predictable.

Third period (February 10-19): reseda or mignonette. The name comes from the Latin verb resedare, 'to calm'. The fragrance of this charming flower placates an agitated spirit and helps to keep sight of the high road and to put one's thoughts in order.

Animals Associated with Aquarius

The ability to change its color makes the chameleon one of the animals that correspond with Aquarius. Like this creature, Aquarius changes behavior, attachments and viewpoints. Not because they are weathervanes that move with every gust of wind, but because life is a continuous becoming and they do not want to remain anchored to just one scheme, one color. For Aquarius, things must never remain static. Aquarius is Air, which is changeable, inconsistent, fluctuating, intangible and elusive. Aquarius has a strong tie with Air which brings them close to birds, particularly the coot, kingfisher, seagull, robin, finch, quail and titmouse, not to mention the bird dedicated to Aquarius, the peacock. Sacred to Saturn and Juno, the peacock's tail, or 'train' in Greek mythology, symbolized the firmament, while in Christian tradition it is a sign of immortality and symbolizes vanity. While, generally speaking, Aquarius is not arrogant or presumptuous, they do have a lot of self-esteem and occasionally don't mind 'strutting'.

Two animals that are apparently opposites, the cat and dog, are also associated with Aquarius. The cat is the symbol of dexterity, ingenuity and cunning, and Aquarius is a master when it comes to astuteness. The cat's sweet and crafty behavior makes it a symbol of falseness and Aquarius is not always an example of absolute sincerity. Telling fibs, feigning and inventing are traits of Aquarius; they are clever at defending untenable opinions, at making even the most improbable statement plausible. Vice versa, Aquarius is also faithful and reliable, just like the dog. If an idea fascinates Aquarius, if a friend gets them involved in something that really affects them deeply, then they will be willing to follow it or him to the ends of the Earth with a constant, sincere and positive presence.

Gemstones Associated with Aquarius

If the rule of Saturn is stronger and Aquarius wants to assimilate the qualities of this planet (cold logic, rationality, detachment, equilibrium, realism and authoritativeness) then they should concentrate on black amber, also known as jet. Particularly sought after in ancient Rome for its protective properties, this stone was usually engraved with symbolic images and used as an amulet. A black amber necklace or jewel lends great mental clarity to the wearer, stimulates sensory vision, and reinforces their work and public image. This stone is easy to work, so Aquarius can carve a figure or symbol dear to them in order to make it even more beneficial. Remember, however, not to give black amber to other people, or let it be touched by too many different hands. Traditionally, it was believed that it put body and soul in contact, protected the wearer's vital space, became 'fond' of its owner and never wanted to be separated from them.

If, on the other hand, the rule of Uranus is stronger and Aquarius wants to assimilate the qualities of this planet (practicality, inventiveness, brilliant intelligence, idealism, opportunism, efficiency, realism, dynamism, and fast reflexes and execution), then they should wear blue sapphire to ward off sadness and hatred and encourage cheerfulness and love. This is a sacred stone for many religions. For example, it symbolizes divine wisdom for Christians, while Buddhists believe that it reinforces devotion and spiritual illumination. The sapphire can be used to diminish individualism in favor of altruism, as well as to rid oneself of blockages that impede freedom and happiness.

If Aquarius wants to combine the qualities of Saturn and Uranus, then they should choose the jacinth stone, which is mostly red and symbolizes faithfulness and pure feelings. Jacinth also reminds us that those born under Aquarius celebrate St. Valentine's Day (February 14): it is a perfect pledge of love for a special person.

Best Food for Aquarius

For Aquarius, which is an Air sign, the most suitable method of cooking is by steaming. It is eminently healthy and keeps the nutrients of the food intact. But Aquarius cannot always steam their food if they are always on the lookout for new flavors, which they are. Aquarius is a sign that likes to be everywhere and not stop in one place for too long. Translated into cooking, this means a variety of food, aromas and dishes so that the Aquarius palate is not bored.

Anatomically, Aquarius is associated with venous circulation, calves and ankles. Good circulation is connected to a balanced diet, physical activity and ingredients such as raspberries, whortleberries, blackberries, cherries, avocados, salmon, green tea and lemon juice. Besides these, there is a little known fruit that is particularly suitable for Aquarius - the sorb apple. This is the fruit of the service tree, astringent at first but sweet when ripe, and rich in vitamin C. It can be eaten after ripening in straw or used to make excellent liqueurs. The Celts and the Germanic tribes considered the sorb, in particular, and apples, in general, to be the food of the gods. Service tree wood was burned by the Druids to invoke spirits.

Also associated with Aquarius is sweet, black licorice, which is traditionally believed to have digestive and refreshing properties. However, those with very high blood pressure should not eat too much of it.

Aquarius is a sign that is always on the move, always in a state of becoming, always caught up in a vision, a project. In order to calm the Aquarius mind and dominate anxiety and nervousness, one should drink a hawthorn tisane. This small, thorny bush with white flowers and bright red fruit regulates one's heartbeat, calms palpitations, reduces stress and helps one to sleep.

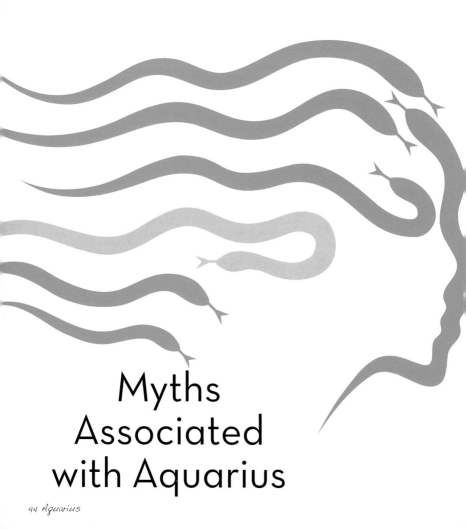

Myths
Associated
with Aquarius

The mythical figure who best represents Aquarius is Icarus, the son of the craftsman and inventor Daedalus. In order to escape from King Minos, Daedalus made wings for himself and his son, which he attached to their bodies with wax. Before taking off, he warned his son not to fly too high, but Icarus, exhilarated by the flight, went higher and higher, soaring too close to the Sun, which melted the wax and caused his wings to fall off, so that he fell into the sea. Like Icarus, at times Aquarius is somewhat foolhardy, unpredictable and disobedient. Like Icarus, they do not care about the risks they take, where they are flying, and which places, confines or situations they traverse. What is important for Aquarius is to fly, soar, and move away from what is already known, from obstacles, barriers, and limits. Woe betide anyone who clips their wings or keeps them in a cage like a canary. Aquarius means freedom, free flight. It also means risk, but they don't mind losing their wings and falling headlong if what they are experiencing is worth the risk.

Aquarius is ruled by Saturn (slow and traditionalist, looking toward the past) and Uranus (fast, impulsive, and dynamic, looking toward the future), and this reminds us of the Roman god Janus, depicted with two faces, looking to both the future and the past, the interior and the exterior. Janus was the god of transition and change, of the beginning and the end, of movement and eternal becoming. His looking at both the past and the future is like Aquarius being ahead of the times. Aquarius is a revolutionary since they are ahead of their time, a visionary because they see things that escape others' notice; they see the future, they imagine it and realize it. Aquarius lives in the present, always directed to the future, because they can predict how the world will change and, by observing the past, learn from it. The prodigious Aquarius inventiveness, the ability to find every possible solution, their talent for originality and their technological ability also liken them to Hephaestus, the god of fire, technology and inventions.

Aquarius Fairy Tale

Lewis Carroll, author of *Alice in Wonderland*, was born under Aquarius. His remarkable imagination came from Aquarius, as did his capacity to create fantastic worlds and situations. It is not easy to summarize this famous tale. Alice follows the White Rabbit and meets various characters and has paradoxical experiences with the Cheshire Cat, the Mad Hatter, the evil Queen of Hearts and many other strange creatures. But, Alice is not frightened. She faces every situation with a spirit of adventure, which is typical of Aquarius. For Aquarius, a monotonous life is hard to endure and they are always on the lookout for new experiences, and are attracted by the unexpected. Life should not be lived with the same rhythms and tasks, but should be seasoned with strange, extravagant, and unpredictable events. Like Alice, Aquarius is ready and willing to follow the White Rabbit into a Wonderland. The Cheshire Cat corresponds to the Aquarius ability to disappear and their chameleon attribute. Aquarius always wants to feel free to come and go as they please. They love to surprise people and to be surprised, to search even though they don't know what they are searching for. When Alice asks the Cheshire Cat which road she should take, he asks her where she wants to go. She replies that she doesn't know, and his retort is "Then it doesn't matter." For Aquarius, life is the triumph of the unpredictable: they would like to leave for London and find themselves in St. Petersburg. They are good at evaluating, preparing and organizing, but they always leave some room for a clever intuition, or for a surprise that will leave them baffled.

Alice eating some cake and becoming enormously tall, then shrinking and growing tall once again, corresponds to the Aquarius ability to change and never be constant. No sooner does someone think he has fully understood Aquarius and has them pigeonholed, than they have already slipped away and become someone else.

PATRIZIA TRONI, trained at the school of Marco Pesatori, writes the astrology columns for Italian magazines *Marie Claire* and *Telepiù*. She has worked in the most important astrology magazines (*Astra, Sirio, Astrella, Minima Astrologica*), she has edited and written the astrology supplement of *TV Sorrisi e Canzoni* and *Chi* for years, and she is an expert not only in contemporary astrology, but also in Arab and Renaissance astrology.

Photo Credits

Archivio White Star pages 28, 34, 38; artizarus/123RF page 20 center; Cihan Demirok/123RF pages 1, 2, 3, 4, 14, 30, 48; Yvette Fain/123RF page 46; file404/123RF page 16 bottom; Olexandr Kovernik/123RF page 42; Valerii Matviienko/123RF pages 8, 12; murphy81/Shutterstock page 44; Igor Nazarenko/123RF page 40; Michalis Panagiotidis/123RF pages 20, 21; tribalium123/123RF page 16; Maria Zaynullina/123RF page 36

WHITE STAR PUBLISHERS

WS White Star Publishers® is a registered trademark property of De Agostini Libri S.p.A.

© 2015 De Agostini Libri S.p.A.
Via G. da Verrazano, 15 · 28100 Novara, Italy
www.whitestar.it · www.deagostini.it

Translation: Richard Pierce · Editing: Norman Gilligan

ISBN 978-88-544-0973-6
1 2 3 4 5 6   19 18 17 16 15

Printed in China